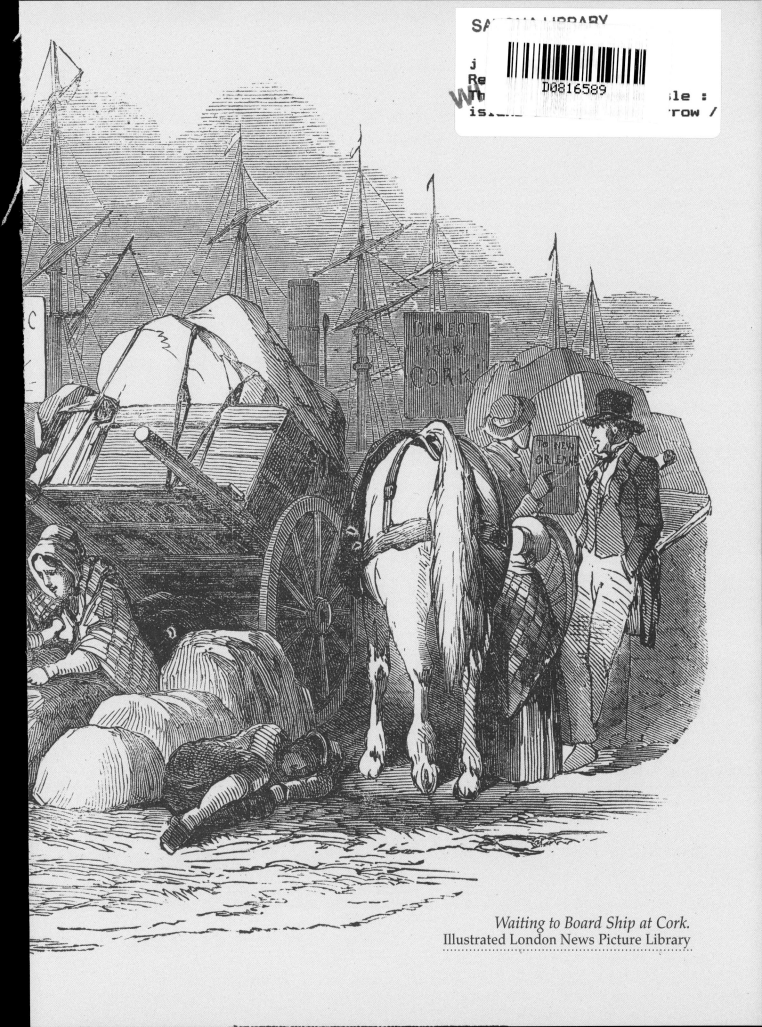

Waiting to Board Ship at Cork.
Illustrated London News Picture Library

Island of
Hope and Sorrow

THE STORY OF GROSSE ÎLE

written by Anne Renaud

Lobster Press ™

Dedicated to my grandparents Emma Mitchell and Gerald Delaney who, in search of a new beginning, left their homelands to forge a life in Canada.

I would like to extend my heartfelt gratitude to the following people who graciously provided their time, knowledge, memories, photographs, artifacts, and support for this book. To Marianna O'Gallagher and Rose Masson Dompierre whose many literary works on the topic of Grosse Île were the cornerstone of my research. Their deep affection for this island, which both women imparted to me through their printed words, set the tone for mine. To my "first readers", historians André Charbonneau, Christine Chartré, Yvan Fortier, and collections manager, Diane Le Brun, of Parks Canada. To site manager, Daniel Villeneuve, and the employees of Grosse Île, in particular, Jo-Anick Proulx, whose assistance in helping me secure photographs and images for this book was invaluable. To Michael Kenneally, Chair in Canadian Irish Studies, Concordia University; Mark McGowan, Principal of the University of St. Michael's College, University of Toronto; Elsbeth Heaman, Department of History, McGill University; Brendan Dinneen, of the Jeanie Johnston (Ireland) Company Ltd.; author John Bryden; and Gail White, of the Westmount Public Library. To my editor at Lobster Press, Meghan Nolan, whose patience and assiduity helped me bring this project to term. Finally, to my childhood friend, Linda Malenfant, for her wisdom and unflagging cheerleading.

Island of Hope and Sorrow: The Story of Grosse Île
Text © 2007 Anne Renaud
Illustrations © 2007 Aries Cheung

Published by Lobster Press™
1620 Sherbrooke Street West, Suites C & D
Montréal, Québec H3H 1C9
Tel. (514) 904-1100 • Fax (514) 904-1101
www.lobsterpress.com

Editors: Alison Fripp and Meghan Nolan
Editorial Assistants: Katie Scott and Olga Zoumboulis
Graphic Design: Olena Lytvyn
Production Manager: Tammy Desnoyers
Illustrations: Aries Cheung

The Canada Council | Le Conseil des Arts
for the Arts | du Canada

The author acknowledges the support of the Canada Council for the Arts, which last year invested $20.1 million in writing and publishing throughout Canada.

We acknowledge the support of the Canada Council for the Arts for our publishing program.

Société
de développement
des entreprises
culturelles

Québec

We acknowledge the support of the government of Québec, tax credit for book publishing, administered by SODEC.

Library and Archives Canada Cataloguing in Publication

Renaud, Anne, 1957-
          Island of Hope and Sorrow : the Story of Grosse Île / Anne Renaud ; Aries Cheung, illustrator.
(Canadian immigration)

ISBN 13 : 978-1-897073-54-4
ISBN 10 : 1-897073-54-2

1. Grosse Île, La (Montmagny, Québec)--History--Juvenile literature.
2. Quarantine--Québec (Province)--Grosse Île, La (Montmagny)--History--
Juvenile literature. 3. Canada--Emigration and immigration--History--
Juvenile literature. I. Cheung, Aries, 1960- II. Title. III. Series: Canadian
immigration (Montréal, Québec)
FC2945.G78R45 2007   j971.4'735   C2006-905108-9

Front cover (from top, moving clockwise): Aerial view of Grosse Île, Parks Canada; Russian immigrant children on Grosse Île in 1912, Lucienne Masson Collection; The Jeanie Johnston in full sail in the summer of 2003, Paul Dolan of FÁS, Tralee; Passengers Act of 1848, The Jeanie Johnston (Ireland) Company Limited.   Printed and bound in Canada.

IMAGINE an island
rising like a hump out of the Saint Lawrence
River. Perched atop a hill on its western-most point, stands a Celtic
cross like a lone soldier on watch. Below, the landscape is dotted
with clusters of trees and shrubs, rocky flats, and weather-worn
buildings imprinted with the passage of time.

Welcome to Grosse Île. Its history tells of hope and hardship for
thousands of people in search of a new homeland, of
caring island workers who welcomed them to their shores, and of
timber ships and deadly diseases. Sadly, for some, Grosse Île
marked the end of a journey. But for most newcomers, this tiny
island was the stepping stone to a new beginning.

This is one of the many stories of the building of Canada.

3

THE TIMBER TRADE

⚓ **The Napoleonic Wars were fought in Europe between 1799 and 1815. Many countries, including England, Russia, and Austria fought against France, whose leader was Napoleon Bonaparte.**

☸ **The Baltic countries border the eastern coast of the Baltic Sea. They include Estonia, Latvia, and Lithuania.**

🌿 **Colonies were settlements of people who left their countries to go live in another land. Hundreds of years ago, France and Britain set up colonies in North America. In the early 1800s, Nova Scotia, New Brunswick, and Upper Canada and Lower Canada were all colonies that were ruled by the British, who won control of them in the Seven Years' War of 1756-1763.**

🗼 **New World was the name given to the continents of South America and North America, after Europeans settled there. First Nations people populated the New World long before France and Britain sent people to establish the colonies. Among these tribal Nations were the Hurons, the Iroquois, the Abenakis, and the Inuit.**

DURING the Napoleonic Wars ⚓, Britain needed timber to build its warships. But a blockade of French ships had cut Britain off from the Baltic countries ☸, which had been its main source of timber for many years.

Turning to its colonies 🌿 in the New World 🗼, Britain found a new supply of timber in the forests of Nova Scotia, New Brunswick, and of Upper and Lower Canada. In winter, workers in the lumber camps would cut down trees and trim them into logs. When spring came, the logs were then tied into rafts, and raftsmen floated them down the rivers to ports. The logs were then untied, loaded onto ships, and sailed across the sea to Britain.

The timber raft. Some rafts were as large as half a kilometer long and carried crews of men that lived on them in small huts. Library and Archives Canada (C-150716)

The British colonies of Nova Scotia, New Brunswick, Upper Canada (southern region of today's province of Ontario) and Lower Canada (southern-eastern region of today's province of Quebec and Labrador).

During the war years and in the years after peace came to Europe, Ireland's population grew enormously. By 1820, this island country was faced with overpopulation and a shortage of farmland. Also, in Britain there were not enough jobs after the war industries shut down. Nor was there enough work for all the soldiers that had been released from military service. Because of this, many Scots, Welsh, English, and mainly Irish were drawn to the sparsely populated colonies of the New World, where it would be possible for them to own farmland and find employment.

Throughout this time, the colonies continued to supply Britain with timber. The wood was used for ties for the railroad, and to make furniture, houses, wagons, and carts. In the colonies, however, there was little demand for European goods. This meant that the cargo holds of timber ships were almost empty when they left Britain.

But this soon changed.

Ship owners saw an opportunity in the hopeful immigrants ⚓ who were eager to travel to the New World. By converting their cargo holds into rows of berths, which were then covered with straw for bedding, they could offer cheap passage across the Atlantic ☸. Timber ships now carried human cargo in their lower decks when they set sail for the colonies.

The journey across the Atlantic usually lasted between six to ten weeks, depending on the winds. In the holds of the timber ships, men, women, and children lay cramped in berths that often held entire families. When the passengers arrived at their destination, the temporary accommodations were taken apart, and the cargo holds were filled with goods and timber for the voyage back to Britain.

As the timber trade grew, so did the port of Quebec. By 1830, it had become the largest and busiest centre for immigration and maritime trade.

HISTORY NOTES

⚓ **Immigrants are people who move from their land of birth to another country.**

☸ **Passengers who paid the lowest fare traveled in the lower decks of the ship, also called steerage. People who could afford to pay the higher fare traveled in small cabins on the ship's upper decks.**

Scotland

Ireland

Wales

England

United Kingdom of Great Britain and Ireland, in the early 19th century, also called the British Isles.

5

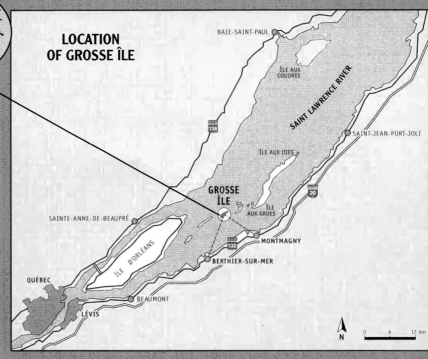

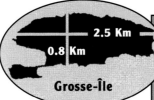

Grosse Île is about two-and-a-half kilometers long and one kilometer wide. It is part of the archipelago, or group of islands, that sits downstream from the port of Quebec. Parks Canada

CHOLERA.

CHOLERA has made its appearance on board several Passenger Ships proceeding from IRELAND to the UNITED STATES OF AMERICA and CANADA and has, in some instances, been very fatal. There can be no doubt that the sea sickness consequent on the rough weather which Ships must encounter, joined to the cold and damp of a sea voyage, will render persons who are not strong more susceptible to the attacks of this disease.

WE strongly recommend that passengers should wrap themselves with as much warm clothing as they can, and especially with flannel, to be worn next the Skin; that they should keep both their clothes and their persons quite clean, and should be careful to keep them so during the entire voyage, - and that they should consume as much solid and wholesome food as they can, in addition to the Ship's allowance on the voyage.

**By Order of
Dr. R. Blennerhassett,
~ Ship's Surgeon.**

As the disease spread, public health notices such as this one were posted aboard ships and throughout the British Isles.
The Jeanie Johnston (Ireland) Company Limited

HISTORY NOTES

⚓ **Asiatic cholera is a disease that people catch from drinking water or eating food that carries the cholera bacteria. Symptoms include spasms, vomiting, and diarrhea, which can lead to severe dehydration and death.**

☸ **Quarantine meant keeping passengers on the island for a period of time in case they might be carrying diseases.**

CHOLERA

IN 1831, Asiatic cholera ⚓ spread across Europe. Health officials in Lower Canada had to quickly find a way to prevent the disease from reaching the colonies. They needed a place where ships could be inspected and passengers could be quarantined ☸ before continuing on to the mainland.

On February 25, 1832, the Assembly of Lower Canada passed a resolution establishing Grosse Île as a quarantine station. The island was the perfect setting because of its size and its surrounding waters, which were deep enough for ships to drop anchor. It sat about fifty kilometers from the port of Quebec, and was on the path of the main shipping routes.

Grosse Île from the officers' quarters. The semaphore is on the far right, on the island's highest point. Library and Archives Canada (C-013656)

In the spring, when the ice thawed on the Saint Lawrence River, teams of workmen and soldiers made their way to Grosse Île. They built a T-shaped post on the island's highest hill to send messages by semaphore to the mainland ✐ . They constructed houses for the doctors, barracks for the soldiers, a hospital shed for the sick passengers, and another shed for the healthy passengers. The island was under the command of the army and cannons were set up near the shore to remind ships that they now needed to stop at Grosse Île before reaching Quebec.

In early May, the island was ready to receive its first wave of newcomers.

HISTORY NOTES

✐ Semaphore is a visual signaling system. To relay messages from Grosse Île to the mainland, a series of T-shaped posts were constructed along the shores of the Saint Lawrence River from Montmagny to Quebec. Each post was set up atop a hill and carried a telescope so the semaphore operators could see the messages and relay them from one post to the next. The messages were made up of coloured flags and canvas balloons that were attached to the moveable arms of the posts. Each flag and balloon had a different meaning, depending on its colour and position.

◀ *Although these cannons were set up on the island to remind ships to stop at Grosse Île, not once did the cannons have to be fired for this purpose.*
Claude Morin Collection

THE FIRST SEASON

WITHIN three weeks after the quarantine island opened, there were already twelve ships anchored at Grosse Île. The arrival of each ship set off a flurry of activity on the island. Usually, each ship was boarded by doctors who determined if there had been any deaths or births during the voyage. They also examined all passengers to see if any were sick and needed to be hospitalized. Because doctors were not sure how cholera spread or what were the symptoms, these examinations were brief and consisted of little more than the doctors looking at each passenger.

After inspection, if there were sick people aboard, soldiers would row small boats out to the ship to collect all the travelers and their belongings and bring them ashore. Passengers were then housed in either the hospital shed, or the shed for the healthy.

Books in which births and deaths on Grosse Île were recorded. Parks Canada

The first installations of the quarantine station on Grosse Île, in 1832. Parks Canada, B. Duchesne, 1996

After a few days, when the sick had recovered and the doctors felt that everyone was well, the ships continued on to Quebec. Before leaving the island, each ship received a certificate of health.

By early June, cholera had made its way to Grosse Île. Few deaths were recorded on the island, but the disease moved inland. Passengers, who doctors thought were healthy, became ill and infected others as they continued on their journey. Throughout the summer and fall, the number of sick grew in the settlements ⚓ .

By November, when it came time to close the island before the ice set in, thousands of newly arrived immigrants and local settlers had died from the disease in Quebec, Montreal, Kingston, and beyond.

[From the Quebec Gazette of June 11.]
THE ASIATIC CHOLERA.—We announced the existence of the CHOLERA at Grosse Isle on Friday.—It is now in this city. Its effects in an American climate are likely to be more severe than in Europe.
  It becomes the duty of all to be vigilant in repelling the ravages of this common destroyer. Cleanliness, temperance, regularity of habits, moderate eating and exercise, and exemption from all excess, are the best preventives.
  The greatest number of deaths are from Champlain street. Three or four deaths have occurred in the upper town. Deaths have been caused in from 5 to 6 hours.
                              Four o'clock, P. M.

Cholera makes its way to the mainland.
Richmond Enquirer, June 22, 1832

◀ *Health Certificate for the Hope, 1833.*
Library and Archives Canada (RG 42, Vol 14)

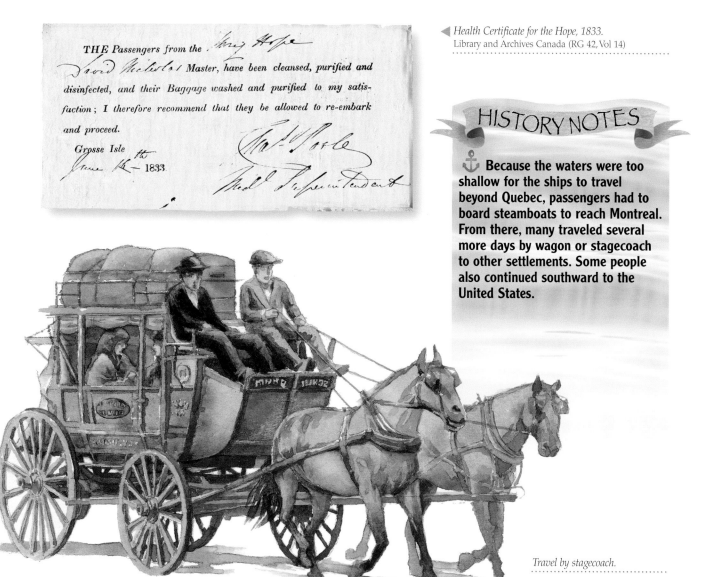

THE Passengers from the *Brig Hope*
David Nicholas Master, have been cleansed, purified and disinfected, and their Baggage washed and purified to my satisfaction; I therefore recommend that they be allowed to re-embark and proceed.
  Grosse Isle
  June 14th — 1833.

HISTORY NOTES

⚓ **Because the waters were too shallow for the ships to travel beyond Quebec, passengers had to board steamboats to reach Montreal. From there, many traveled several more days by wagon or stagecoach to other settlements. Some people also continued southward to the United States.**

Travel by stagecoach.

1833-1845

WITH the exception of a second devastating outbreak of cholera in 1834, during which 844 people were hospitalized and 264 died, activities on the island were relatively quiet in the years that followed. Passengers arrived sick with smallpox, measles, and other diseases, but their numbers were small and few deaths were recorded on Grosse Île.

At the beginning of each season of operation, steamboats filled with soldiers and workers, doctors and nurses, as well as priests, would leave the port of Quebec for Grosse Île. During the season, soldiers and workers repaired the buildings and built new ones. They rowed out to the ships to collect the passengers and bring them to shore. Doctors and nurses took care of the sick, and priests baptized newborn babies, performed burials, and spent long hours comforting patients in hospital.

Healthy immigrants filled part of their days taking walks, or writing entries in their journals and letters to family members they had left behind. Along the shores, children helped their parents cook meals over wood fires or wash their clothing and bedding in the Saint Lawrence River.

A priest baptizing a baby.

Washing clothing and bedding in the river.

What a letter home might have looked like.

Aboard the ships that continued to cross the Atlantic from the British Isles, the routine was similar. Steerage passengers prepared their meals huddled around the cooking fire on the upper deck. Much of their time was spent cleaning their sleeping quarters down below. Some passengers traveled with their fiddles, flutes, and other instruments, which provided entertainment.

In the fall, when the ships stopped coming, Grosse Île emptied once again. During the winter months, only a few workers remained on the island as caretakers.

Grosse Île had survived its first years as a quarantine island, but more frightening times were to come.

Re-creation of life aboard the Jeanie Johnston. Some passengers traveled with their instruments and provided entertainment for the other travelers. The Jeanie Johnston (Ireland) Company Limited

On Ship. Illustrated London News Picture Library

SUMMER OF SORROW

IN THE autumn of 1845, Ireland's potato crops became infected with blight, a plant disease that turned the vegetables to black mush. At the time, this was not considered unusual because it had occurred in previous years. But, the potato crops of the following fall harvests were no better ⚓ . For many Irish farmers, the choice was clear. They could remain in Ireland and face starvation, disease, and death, or cross the ocean to the New World. Immigration had now become an act of desperation, their last hope for survival ☸ .

In the ports of England and Ireland, groups of starving Irish gathered on the docks and waited to board the ships headed westward. Clutching all their possessions, which for many families often fit into one trunk, they made their way up the gangplanks and down into the cargo holds.

Passengers were required to bring their own bedding, cooking pots, and utensils. Ship captains had to provide them with water and limited portions of food, or rations, which could include rice, meat, molasses, tea, flour, and sugar. However, not all captains did. This meant that by the time the ships arrived at their destination, passengers were often no more than skin and bones.

Immigrant's trunk. ▲
L. Malenfant

HISTORY NOTES

⚓ **About one-third of the Irish were farmers.** Most were tenants on land they rented from landlords. Farmers raised sheep for wool and cows to produce milk for cheese and butter. They grew crops of potatoes, as well as wheat, rye, and barley. Farmers and their families lived mainly on their potato crops to feed themselves. They sold their remaining products to other countries to pay the rent to their landlords.

☸ **In 1847, the cost to travel from Ireland to the colonies was about £3,** which was a very large sum of money at that time. Many Irish immigrants who were settled in the colonies sent money or pre-paid tickets to their relatives back home in Ireland, so they could join them. This was called chain-migration.

Re-creation of Irish immigrants inside the cargo hold of the Jeanie Johnston. Author's Collection

With chamber pots or buckets used as toilets, a stifling smell rose from the crowded cargo holds. Added to this was the stench from seasick passengers and overall filth due to insufficient supplies of clean water. In stormy weather, the hatches were closed, leaving little air and no light to penetrate the holds. Soon, many passengers fell sick with typhus, also called ship fever 🪱. The ships became known as "coffin ships," on which thousands died en route to the New World and were laid to rest in the ocean 🗼.

On May 14, 1847, the *Syria*, the first of the ships carrying the new wave of Irish immigrants, arrived at Grosse Île from Liverpool, England. Of the ship's 245 passengers, 125 were sick with typhus and nine had died during the 46-day crossing. Within a day of the *Syria*'s arrival, Grosse Île had recorded its first death of the season when four-year-old Ellen Kane died of ship fever.

STRICTLY FORBIDDEN!

FOR *the safety of the vessel and her entire company and crew the following items and activities are strictly forbidden below decks at all times.*

1. Smoking.
2. Naked Flames & Candles.
3. Lighting of Fires.
4. Fighting
5. Swearing
6. Gambling
7. Spitting
8. Alcoholic Beverages.

~by order of
JAMES ATTRIDGE,
Master of the Jeanie Johnston.

Notice of rules posted in the cargo holds of ships.
The Jeanie Johnston (Ireland) Company Limited

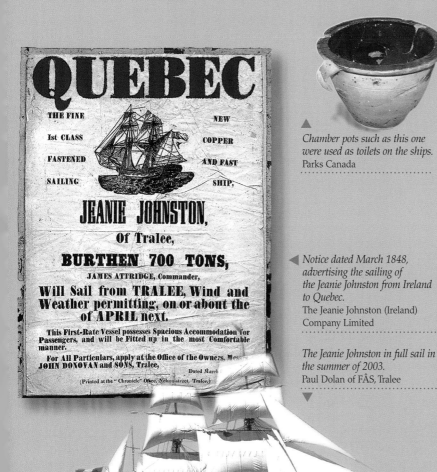

Chamber pots such as this one were used as toilets on the ships.
Parks Canada

Notice dated March 1848, advertising the sailing of the Jeanie Johnston from Ireland to Quebec.
The Jeanie Johnston (Ireland) Company Limited

The Jeanie Johnston in full sail in the summer of 2003.
Paul Dolan of FÁS, Tralee

HISTORY NOTES

🪱 Typhus is passed on from one person to another by lice or fleas. People with the disease develop high fevers, as well as a skin rash that covers their bodies.

🗼 The *Jeanie Johnston* distinguishes herself from the "coffin ships." Built in Quebec in 1847 by noted shipbuilder John Munn, she was sold to Nicholas Donovan of Ireland in 1848. During her sixteen crossings between Ireland and the New World from 1848 to 1856, not one passenger died of ship fever. This is because the ship's doctor insisted that hatches be opened whenever possible. He also encouraged passengers to take a walk on deck every day for exercise and fresh air. To honour the *Jeanie Johnston*'s history, the ship was re-created and sailed to North America from Ireland in 2003.

Quarantine passage, 1847. Parks Canada, B.Duchesne, 1996

By May 21, thirty ships were anchored near Grosse Île. Like a string of beads, they stretched for several kilometers down the Saint Lawrence River. Having changed little since its first year of operation, Grosse Île could not cope with the flood of Irish immigrants. The chapels and the sheds for the healthy were quickly converted into hospitals. Carpenters were sent to the island to build coffins as well as more sheds for the healthy. Hundreds of army tents were set up to shelter the sick and dying who were often placed two and three to a bed. In July alone, over 15,000 immigrants were quarantined on the island. Of these, 1,700 were sick and thirty people were dying every day ⚓ .

Before long, typhus traveled inland to the settlements. Wooden "fever sheds" were built along the river in Montreal's Point Saint Charles neighbourhood to house the hundreds of sick immigrants who arrived daily from the port of Quebec. Most people refused to approach the sick for fear of catching their disease. Some, however, in particular priests and nuns, bravely tended to them.

HISTORY NOTES

⚓ When it opened in 1832, Grosse Île was prepared to hold approximately 1,000 immigrants: 800 healthy and 200 sick. During its first years of operation, the island's medical staff cared for an average of 390 sick passengers per season. However, of all its years of operation, 1847 would bring the greatest number of immigrants to Grosse Île. By the end of the season, Grosse Île had recorded 8,691 sick passengers, of which 3,238 had died on the island, while thousands more had perished before reaching its shores.

Coffins being buried in a mass grave on the island. Parks Canada, Daniel Rainville, 1997

When Grosse Île closed for the season in early November 1847, the grim tally of men, women, and children buried on the island was more than 5,000. Among the children who survived, more than 1,000 were orphans. Many of them were adopted by French-speaking families in and around Quebec.

The seasons of 1848 and 1849 brought more immigrants to Grosse Île, though in much lower numbers than 1847. By then the small island was better prepared ☸ .

When Montreal's Victoria Bridge (above) was being built in the 1850s, the workers, many of them immigrants, came across a mass grave of thousands of Irish who had died of typhus in the fever sheds. In 1859, the workers placed a large stone, pulled from the bed of the Saint Lawrence River, at the entrance of the bridge to mark their grave.
Library and Archives Canada (C-089671)

Top: Stone commemorating Irish immigrants who died of typhus. Le Monde Illustré, August 10, 1895, Bibliothèque et Archives nationales du Québec

PASSENGERS ACT – 1848
ABSTRACT OF THE QUEEN'S ORDER IN COUNCIL FOR PRESERVING ORDER AND SECURING CLEANLINESS AND VENTILATION ON BOARD OF BRITISH SHIPS CARRYING PASSENGERS TO NORTH AMERICA. Prepared by Her Majesty's Colonial Land and Emigration Commissioners, in pursuance of the 13th section of the Act 11th Victoria cap.6.

1. Every passenger to rise at 7 a.m., unless otherwise permitted by the Surgeon; or if no Surgeon, by the Master.
2. Breakfast from 8 to 9 a.m., dinner at 1 p.m. supper at 6 p.m.
3. Passengers to be in their beds by 10 p.m.
4. Fires to be lighted by the passenger's cook at 7 a.m., and then kept alight by him until 7 p.m.; then to be extinguished, unless otherwise directed by the Master, or required for the use of the sick.
5. The Master to determine the order in which the passengers shall be entitled to the use of a the fires for cooking. The cook to take care that this order preserved.
6. Three safety lamps to be lit at dusk; one to be kept burning all the night in the main hatchway, the two others may be extinguished at 11 p.m.
7. No naked light to be allowed at any other time or on any account.
8. The passengers when dressed, to roll up their beds, to sweep the decks (including the space under the bottom of the births) and to throw the dirt overboard.
9. Breakfast not to commence till this is done.
10. The sweepers for the day to be taken in rotation from the males above 14, in the proportion of five for every one hundred passengers.
11. Duties of the sweepers to be to clean the ladders, hospitals, and the round houses, to sweep the decks after every meal, and to dry-holystone and scrape them after breakfast.
12. But the occupant of each birth to see that his own berth is well brushed out.
13. The beds to be well shaken and aired on deck, and the bottom boards if not fixtures, to be removed and dry-scrubbed and taken on deck at least twice a-week.
14. Two days in the week to be appointed by the Master as washing days, but no clothes to be washed or dried between decks.
15. The coppers and cooking vessels to be cleaned every day.
16. The scuttles and stern ports, if any, to be kept open (weather permitting) from 7a.m. to 10 p.m., and the hatches at all hours.
17. Hospitals to be established, with an area, in ships carrying 100 passengers, of not less than 48 superficial feet, with two or four bed-berths, and, in ships carrying 200 passengers, of not less than 120 superficial feet, with six bed-berths.
18. On Sunday the passengers to be mustered at 10 a.m., when they will be expected to appear in clean and decent apparel. The day to be observed as religiously as circumstances will admit.
19. No spirits or gunpowder to be taken on board by any passenger. Any that may be discovered to be taken into custody of the Master till the expiration of the voyage.
20. No loose hay or straw to be allowed below.
21. No smoking to be allowed between decks.
22. All gambling, fighting, riotous or quarrelsome behaviour, swearing and violent language to be at once put a stop to. Swords or other offensive weapons, as soon as the passengers embark, to be placed in the custody of the Master.
23. No sailors to remain on the passenger deck among the passengers except on duty.
24. No passenger to go to the ship's cookhouse without special permission from the Master, nor to remain in the forecastle among the sailors on any account.

By order of the Commissioners,
S. WALCOTT, Secretary
Colonial Land and Emigration Office,
9, Park Street, Westminster, April, 1848.

Following the summer of 1847, changes were made to the Passengers Act in 1848 to ensure cleanliness and prevent the spread of typhus and other diseases aboard the ships.
The Jeanie Johnston (Ireland) Company Limited

HISTORY NOTES

☸ A famine is a great shortage of food. The Irish potato famine, which lasted from 1845 to 1849, is the most tragic event in Ireland's history. During this period, two million people left their country, and one million died of starvation in their homeland. By 1850, Ireland had lost a third of its population in half a decade.

CENTRE   EAST

WEST

After the tragedy of 1847, the island was divided in three sections. Parks Canada

HISTORY NOTES

⚓ On July 1, 1867, the Dominion of Canada was created through the British North America Act. It included the colonies of Upper and Lower Canada, which in 1840 were united to form the province of Canada, as well as the colonies of Nova Scotia and New Brunswick. These colonies now became the four provinces of Quebec, Ontario, Nova Scotia, and New Brunswick. The land between Ontario and the colony of British Columbia belonged to the Hudson's Bay Company. This land was soon purchased by the government to ensure the country's expansion. Manitoba, Canada's fifth province, was created in 1870, along with the Northwest Territories. The colony of British Columbia became the country's sixth province in 1871 after Prime Minister Sir John A. Macdonald promised to build a railway that would reach from east to west.

⚙ Canada Day is celebrated on July 1 because the Dominion, or territory, of Canada was created on that day, back in 1867. Canada Day was first established in 1879 and was called Dominion Day. The name was changed to Canada Day on October 27, 1982.

FOLLOWING the tragic events of 1847, many changes were made on Grosse Île. On the eastern end of the island, the newly built sheds for the healthy were now converted into hospital sheds. This was done to create a greater distance between the sick and the healthy immigrants who were now housed in the western part of the island. A washhouse was built where people could clean their clothes by boiling them in cast iron cauldrons over open fireplaces and rinsing them in wooden sinks. Another small building was built to house a brick oven. There, bedding, which for many passengers was a canvas bag filled with horse hair or feathers, could be exposed to high temperatures for disinfection. Wells were dug to retrieve water, and there was now a school on the island.

Out on the ocean, ships that until then had been powered by wind and sail were being replaced with steamships, shortening the travel time at sea. While immigrants arriving in Quebec were still mainly from the British Isles, ships from Germany and the Scandinavian countries of Sweden, Denmark, and Norway were now crossing the Atlantic ⚓ ⚙ .

R.M.S. Corsican
Dimensions—
Length, 500 ft.
Breadth, 61 ft.
Tonnage, 11,419

▲ *Postcard of the S.S. Corsican. S.S. stands for steamship.* L. Lovegrove

▶ *Immigrants on dock awaiting departure.* Library and Archives Canada (C-006556)

End of the Napoleonic Wars	Outbreak of cholera epidemic in India	Cholera epidem reaches Europ
1815	1827	1831

OPENING OF THE WEST

THE 1870s and 1880s brought a new wave of immigrants to Quebec. Russian Jews escaping pogroms 🖋 in their native country were making their way to Germany's ports to cross the Atlantic. Mennonites were also fleeing Russia to avoid the country's policy of forced military service 🗼. In addition, Icelanders were in search of a new homeland after a volcanic eruption devastated their country.

By the mid 1880s, the 4,600-kilometer-long Canadian Pacific Railway opened, linking Canada from coast to coast ☸. Steam trains now carried newly arrived settlers westward across the continent.

In the late 1890s and early 1900s, Canadian agents were sent to Europe to persuade people to come and populate the West. They put up posters offering free land on which to build farms. In Britain, maps of Canada were distributed in schools, along with atlases.

"The Most Fertile Country in the World," September 1909: One of the posters used to encourage immigration to western Canada.
Library and Archives Canada (C-126299)

Scottish immigrants on a train heading for the West. Library and Archives Canada (PA-010391)

HISTORY NOTES

🖋 **Pogroms were organized attacks or killings of groups of people, especially Jews.**

🗼 **Mennonites are Christians who believe that it is wrong to fight wars. They refuse to serve in the military.**

☸ **In 1845, 18-year-old Sandford Fleming left Scotland and sailed for Quebec on the *Brilliant*. Fleming went on to design Canada's first postage stamp, the "three-penny beaver," which was issued in 1851. He was the chief engineer in the construction of the Canadian Pacific Railway and also invented the universal system of standard time.**

Canada's first postage stamp.
Canada Post Corporation (1851), Reproduced with Permission; Library and Archives Canada (POS-000033)

Opening of the Grosse Île quarantine station	Potato crops in Ireland are destroyed by blight	Canada becomes a nation	The last spike is driven into the last rail of the Canadian Pacific Railway
1832	1845-1849	1867	1885

Throughout the end of the 19th century, Grosse Île underwent many more changes. Under the direction of Dr. Frederick Montizambert, a disinfection building was constructed that housed showers for the immigrants and steam chambers to decontaminate clothing and belongings. Also, upon arrival, sick passengers were brought to the hospital by ambulance, which was a horse-drawn covered wagon made of wood.

Methods of communication improved as well. The island was now connected to Quebec by telegraph wire. This allowed the port to be notified in advance of ship arrivals ⚓ . Parts of the island were also connected by the telephone. This meant that doctors could now phone the hospital to instruct the medical staff and inquire about their patients.

One of the telephones once used on Grosse Île. Claude Morin Collection

Dr. Montizambert was Medical Superintendent of Grosse Île from 1869-1899. In 1899, he became Canada's first Director General of Public Health. He created and put into practice disinfection methods throughout Canada and was responsible for the administration of the country's quarantine stations. He also helped convince the government to establish a Department of Health. Dr. Montizambert died in 1929 and was inducted in the Canadian Medical Hall of Fame in 2001.
Library and Archives Canada (Item no. 2473, Accession No. 1936-270)

HISTORY NOTES

⚓ Telegraph messages were sent by Morse code, which consisted of dots and dashes that replaced each letter of the alphabet. These dots and dashes were tapped out by a telegraph operator in a series of short and long sounds that were sent along electric telegraph wires. The sounds were then decoded into words and sentences by another telegraph operator, usually many miles away, who received the message.

Many members of the Masson family and their descendants were island workers on Grosse Île. Pierre (Pit) Masson was the ambulance driver from 1904 to 1937. When the sick passengers arrived on the island, he would pick them up and take them to the hospital.
Claude Morin Collection

THE 20th CENTURY

IN THE EARLY years of the 20th century, people continued to flow into Canada by way of Quebec City.

The prospect of affordable farmland brought Ukrainians and Poles who settled in the newly created provinces of Saskatchewan and Alberta. In addition, groups of Russian Doukhobors ☸ fleeing oppression in their country sought land and freedom in the West. Many Italians in search of employment remained in the East to become miners and railway workers. Newcomers often did the most backbreaking and dangerous work. They built roads and sewer systems, planted explosives for railroads and quarries, and worked in steel mills and dye factories. They used the skills they had developed in their homelands to work as barbers and cobblers, street vendors, and traveling repairmen. Some men and women worked as tailors and seamstresses making clothing for Toronto's T. Eaton Co.

By now, conditions had greatly improved aboard the steamships as well as on Grosse Île. Among the many new buildings on the island were the first, second, and third class hotels built between 1892 and 1914 for the quarantined passengers. These hotels corresponded to the different levels of comfort in which people now traveled. Generators were built to provide electricity, and a second floor was added to the disinfection building, providing more shower facilities. Roomier, two-storey dwellings stood where small, white-washed board structures had once housed Grosse Île's employees. At the end of 1915, the island also had a vaccination and medical examination office, a residence for the nurses, bakeries, as well as a plumbing and carpentry workshop. Communication with the mainland was now done by wireless telegraph, as well as by telephone 🖋 .

Timothy Eaton immigrated to Canada from Ireland in 1854 at the age of 20. In 1869, he opened a small dry-goods store in Toronto. He later developed the concept of the department store and the mail order catalogue in Canada. At the time of his death in 1907, he had laid the foundation for the Eaton business empire. For many decades, his name was on a chain of department stores all across Canada. Used with the permission of Sears Canada Inc.; City of Toronto Archives

HISTORY NOTES

☸ **Doukhobors are members of a Russian Christian movement. Like the Mennonites, they refuse to serve in the military because they believe that war is wrong.**

🖋 **The wireless telegraph allowed for ship-to-shore and ship-to-ship communication. In the early morning hours of April 15, 1912, the telegraph operator on Grosse Île picked up distress messages. They were from a ship, the *S.S. Titanic*, which had hit an iceberg off the coast of Newfoundland.**

▶

Immigrants building Toronto's sewer system. City of Toronto Archives

Georges Bilodeau was one of the engineers in charge of the disinfection of the hospital material and the belongings of the sick passengers.
Claude Morin Collection

Coat button of the uniform of the quarantine station employees. Parks Canada

While most island employees only worked from May to November, about a dozen families now lived year-round on Grosse Île. These families kept animals, such as cows, chickens, goats, and pigs, which provided them with eggs, milk, and meat in winter. During the months of snow and cold, the islanders often made their way around Grosse Île with snowshoes and skis. It was also at this time that the men cut blocks of ice from the Saint Lawrence River for the icehouses ⚓ .

Although they often had to rely on interpreters to communicate, island workers felt a deep kinship with the newcomers. At the sound of the ambulance bell announcing the arrival of sick immigrants to the island, children in the classroom said a prayer for their speedy recovery. Moreover, the graves of immigrants buried at Grosse Île were lovingly tended by the island dwellers.

HISTORY NOTES

⚓ **At the turn of the 20th century, the home refrigerator was a new invention and few people owned one. On Grosse Île, families kept their food in small wooden buildings called icehouses. The icehouses were built partially underground and stored large blocks of ice that sat on beds of sawdust for insulation.**

Fragment of a doll found in the village sector.
Parks Canada

Top right: *In the spring, the number of schoolchildren increased greatly with the arrival of the seasonal employees. During the winter months, only the dozen or so who remained on the island with their families attended school. The teacher, whose home was the small schoolhouse, remained on the island year-round. The island workers' children were taught up until grade seven, before having to go to school on the mainland.* Ivy Percoco Collection

Children of island workers playing on the shores of Grosse Île at low tide. Martineau-Boulet Collection

During the economic boom years of 1900 to 1914, arrivals at Quebec numbered more than 1.5 million. This stream of people, however, was reduced to a trickle from 1914 to 1918 while World War I raged on in Europe. But with the end of World War I, the tide rose again bringing Bulgarians, Romanians, Norwegians, Czechoslovakians, and Yugoslavians to Canada. Ships from the British Isles also brought a growing number of "home children" ☸ .

By the 1930s, however, the dust bowl ✐ in the Prairies and the economic depression that followed the stock market crash of 1929 🗼 brought fewer ships to Quebec. The changes in migration patterns and the opening of other ports of entry, particularly on the Pacific Coast, also contributed to the decrease. These factors, coupled with Quebec's new hospital, which was now well equipped to deal with contagious diseases, left little need for the quarantine station to remain open. And so, in the fall of 1937, the island officially closed after 105 years of operation.

GAZETTE, MONTREAL, WEDNESDAY, OCTOBER 30, 1929.

THE MARKET · CRASH IN MARKET OF RECORD SIZE · STEEL DECLA EXTRA DI

Stock market crash headline.
"The Montreal Gazette,"
October 30, 1929

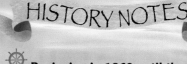
☸ **Beginning in 1869 until the early 1930s, thousands of "home children" crossed the Atlantic from Great Britain with the hope of a better life in Canada. These children were called "home children" because they came from orphanages or "homes" that cared for them. When they arrived in Canada, the children were placed with families, mostly farmers, to work.**

✐ **The "dust bowl" was the name given to large areas of farmland and pastureland in the Canadian Prairies that were ruined by drought and dust storms in the 1930s.**

🗼 **During the 1920s, people invested large amounts of money in the stock market. The more shares people bought, the higher the value of the shares rose. The higher the value of their shares rose, the more money people borrowed from the banks in order to buy even more shares. On October 24, 1929, the share prices fell dramatically. Thousands of people lost their savings, and banks that had lent money were now in debt.**

☸ **Shortly after Elsie and John Lake's father left to fight in World War I, their mother died of pneumonia. In time, the children were placed in the Children's Emigration Home in Birmingham, England. Elsie was six years old and her brother John was ten when they sailed from England on May 19, 1922. They arrived at the port of Quebec aboard the *S.S. Montcalm* and were put on a train for New Brunswick. Elsie and her brother were separated when they arrived in Moncton and were sent to work in two different towns. Elsie did not see her brother again for eight years. Sadly, not all the families Elsie worked for treated her well. Her first Christmas stocking was filled with potato peelings, while the stockings of the family's children were filled with candies and toys. Fortunately, other people for whom Elsie worked were more kindhearted.**

Elsie and her four-year-old brother, John, with their mother, Elizabeth.
Elsie Hathaway Collection

A SECRET MISSION

FOR ALMOST five years following the closing of the quarantine station, Grosse Île was a deserted island. But in the summer of 1942, a boat carrying a group of scientists traveled to its shores. Canada was at war, and Grosse Île would now be a part of the country's new research program on biological weapons ⚓ .

Soon after the beginning of the Second World War, Canadian scientists became worried that the country's enemies might spread germs that would cause diseases in farm animals and people. Because of these fears, parts of Grosse Île's disinfection buildings and hospital were converted into laboratories. There, scientists worked on developing a vaccine for rinderpest, a deadly cattle disease for which there was no cure. They also conducted research on bacteria that Canada and its allies might use against their enemies.

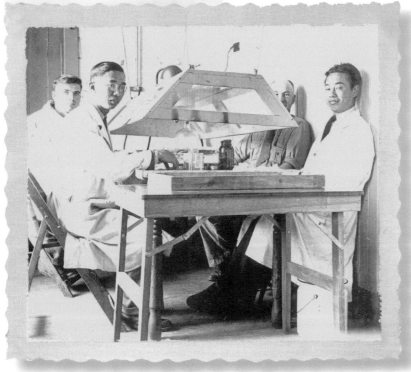

Veterinarians and doctors attending educational sessions on Grosse Île. Fonds Claude Morin

After the war, the laboratories were dismantled. In 1957, the island was taken over by the Department of Agriculture to study animal diseases. Beginning in 1965, Grosse Île served once again as a quarantine station, but this time, for animals. Cattle imported from Europe and elsewhere were quarantined on the island before joining the herds on the mainland. Veterinarians from around the world came to study on Grosse Île, which had become a famous centre for research on animal diseases.

A scientist conducting an experiment. Fonds Claude Morin

Celtic cross is inaugurated on Grosse Île	World War I	Stock market crashes
1909	1914–1918	1929

In Their Memory

IN 1974, the Historic Sites and Monuments Board of Canada recommended that Grosse Île be designated an historic site. The island would be preserved as a place of memory to honour the immigrants who traveled to Canada during the 19th and early 20th centuries, in particular, the Irish who died in 1847. As well, the site would recognize the role the quarantine island played in the building of Canada from 1832 to 1937.

Grosse Île, which Agriculture Canada turned over to Parks Canada for caretaking, opened to the public in the spring of 1988. Today, many of the buildings, including the lazaretto, also called the smallpox hospital, still stand. There are also sites and symbols that pay tribute to those whose lives ended on the island.

The island's oldest commemorative artifact is the Monument to Physicians built around 1853 by Grosse Île's first medical superintendent, Dr. George Douglas. It bears the names of the doctors who died while caring for the sick immigrants.
Parks Canada, L. Delisle

This children's shoe was unearthed in 1996 during archaeological digs on the island. It was found near the lazaretto, which housed the healthy Irish immigrants during the summer of 1847, and is believed to date back to that period.
Parks Canada, J. Beardsell

Built in 1909 by the Ancient Order of Hibernians, an organization made up of Irish Roman Catholics, the Celtic cross stands approximately fifteen meters high. An inscription at the base of the granite monument tells the sad story in English, French, and Gaelic of the Irish immigrants who fled their homeland during the Great Famine. Parks Canada, H. Boucher

The lazaretto is the only remaining shed built in 1847. Clear squares of plastic protect wall drawings made over the years by immigrants. One room, which was painted in 1904, is entirely red, and the windows are covered in red panes of glass. It was believed that the colour red, in addition to shielding patients from sunlight, would help cure smallpox. The building was renovated in 1997 and 1998 to make it safe for visitors. Freddy Masson Collection

Closing of the Grosse Île quarantine station	World War II	Grosse Île is recognized as an historic site	Opening of Grosse Île to the public by Parks Canada
1937	1939–1945	1974	1988

LEGACY

TODAY, Grosse Île and the Irish Memorial National Historic Site of Canada, as it is now known, still bears witness to the passage of so many of our ancestors. When you visit this small island, remember them as you retrace their footsteps.

The Irish cemetery is the final resting place of more than 6,000 immigrants who died in 1832, 1834, and 1847. Parks Canada

Located near the Irish cemetery is the Grosse Île Memorial. Engraved on glass panels around the circular-shaped stone structure are the names of immigrants who died on the island and of the people who died caring for them. More than 1,500 tiny ships are also engraved in the glass, one for each immigrant whose identity is unknown. Parks Canada, X. Bonacorsi

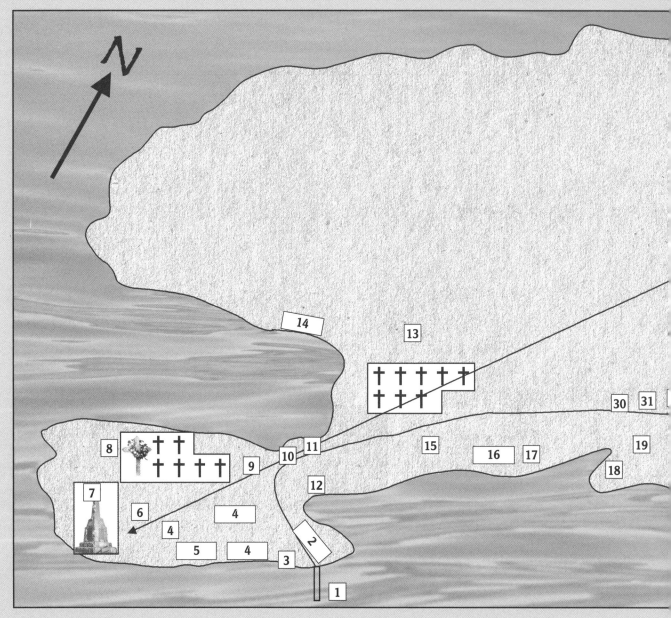

1. Western wharf
2. Generator, pump, showers, and disinfection equipment
3. House for wharf keeper
4. Hotels for immigrants
5. Workshop for plumber
6. Water reservoir
7. Celtic cross
8. Irish cemetery
9. House for electrician
10. House for police
11. Guard post

12. House for doctor
13. Central cemetery
14. Quarters for Grosse Île sailors and their families
15. Anglican presbytery
16. Anglican chapel
17. House for engineer of public works
18. Cannons
19. House for doctor
20. Central quarters
21. Community barn
22. House for employees of public works
23. Marconi station